Prepping Hacks

I0422208

Beginner Tips to Survive Almost Anything

By Bill Shepherd

© 2015

Are You Prepared? For almost anything?

You know you need to be prepared. But maybe you don't know where to start? Maybe you consider yourself an expert prepper already. Maybe you're just a beginner. No matter how long you've been prepping, we all make mistakes. It's natural. It's human. But there are ways you can learn from others and avoid the same mistakes that we all make.

With this book, you'll learn how to be prepared for almost any event and how to survive for as long as you need to!

If you are interested in learning how to protect your family from any and all of the inevitable disasters that could potentially happen, this book is your first step to learning how to prepare for any emergency situation.

Don't wait - Get started today!

What is prepping and who is it for? Prepping is a desire to succeed in and be prepared for a survival situation, ranging from natural disasters to economic collapse and any other unfortunate event – even zombies. Stocking up on food, medicine and survival gear is your insurance against tragedy. Regardless of your level of disposable income or living situation, you can definitely take steps to protect yourself from disaster – prepping is for EVERYONE.

How do we begin to cover this vast topic and all there is to consider? It can seem overwhelming, that's for sure. That's why we're cutting straight to the chase with this book: Prepping Hacks. These are the things you can start on right now, today.

The most important thing you can do to protect yourself, your property and your loved ones is to just start. Purchase and store what you can. Most folks are not made of money and living on acres, but just by starting to prepare and think like a prepper will put you light years ahead of someone with more resources but no concern for entertaining the idea of a survival situation.

On a Budget?

No matter who you are, you have a budget. A budget of time, space and money – there's never enough, is there? How can you consider yourself a prepper when you can't afford an AR-15? What if you don't have room to store giant barrels of grain like the guy you saw on TV? And who has the time to learn how to craft their own bullets? When you prepare for a survival situation, you are hoping to *survive* the event.

You can't and you won't have every conceivable survival supply item on the market. There really aren't any set standards or requirements for you to meet, and any steps you take are better than none. Any thought that you've given a possible scenario will help you far more than any gadget. Indeed, there are many gadgets and gizmos out there which are specifically marketed towards preppers in hopes of cashing in on this craze.

It's up to you to evaluate what is truly useful for your particular situation, and discover when there are cheaper alternatives that can still get the job done. You don't need anything fancy, you just need something that *works*. So, you don't have room for a man-sized gun safe? You probably don't need one, either. Focus on filling up the little spaces in your apartment with nonperishable food and water.

Maybe you've got some spots left under the bed, or you could add shelf space to your laundry room. If you don't have a lot of time, that's fine. Use your time *wisely*. Read about prepping and search the internet for tips, advice and hacks to make your life easier. It's okay to be busy, prepping doesn't *have* to be a fulltime commitment. It's a lifelong endeavor, where you can watch your skills and supplies build slowly over time.

You probably wanted to start prepping to calm some anxiety about a possible doomsday scenario. Let's not also accumulate anxiety over how your preps measure up, as well.

Bugging In or Out

Depending on the situation you find yourself in, it may be safer to remain in your home or you may have to abandon it. This is the choice between bugging in and bugging out. Bugging in might be a much more appealing and comfortable proposition. You will be surrounded by all your belongings, a comfortable bed, changes of clothes and four walls to protect you. In this space, you enjoy your family photo albums, houseplants and hobbies.

You are comforted by your familiarity with the area and the deadbolt on the front door. Who wouldn't want to remain in the comfort of their own home? Leaving it all behind is probably the *last* thing anyone would want to do. But there may come a time where it is unwise or even deadly to shelter in place. What if there were approaching wildfires? What if a viral outbreak spread far and wide throughout your community inducing riots and pandemonium?

You might even be doing just fine at home, but you have run out of food and need to scavenge an ever expanding area. You may have ridden out the apocalypse, but things have gotten so bad that you must head out to find survivors to help rebuild society. If things get too heated, you may have to bug out – preferably to a secondary location previously decided upon.

Bugging out could mean leaving in your vehicle, but many disaster scenarios could bring traffic to a standstill. There is always the possibility that you will have to escape on foot, off the beaten path away from other people. Bugging out means you will be preparing to think on your feet and live off the land, as seen in so many survivor shows on television.

Sometimes you can pick up some great advice from these programs, but at the end of the day the hosts still have camera crews and medics following them around. Surviving in the outdoors is not something to be taken lightly. Try it out for a few days if you can. Head out for an extended camping session with your bugout bag and practice the survival techniques you picked up.

Something as essential as building a fire or a shelter is a lot more work than people realize. If you cannot reliably provide yourself with food, shelter and water for at least 3 days, you know that you have some work to do. Be sure to study survival manuals and outdoor guides, just in case you're ever forced into the wilderness.

Threat Levels

When it hits the fan, and you are ready to tough it out, your actions will widely be determined by the threat level you are facing. When there's a bad thunderstorm outside, we might tune in to weather alerts, grab a few candles and stay away from the windows. And yeah, if a giant herd of walking dead was lumbering down your street you might want to grab your bag and your shotgun and get the heck out, heading for an unpopulated area.

The duration of these events are going to be different. You can ride out the storm for the night, and if the fabled zombies infect enough people you may be on the run for months or even years. An event with minimal impact and short duration will have you reacting differently than a severe threat that will require self-reliance for an extended period of time.

Any citizen, at the very least, should have enough supplies to see them through the immediate crisis of a minimal event and possibly three to five days after. Any budget should allow you to stow away some extra food and water. You don't need anything fancy or expensive, you are covering the bare necessities like sustenance and hygiene.

Once you have collected enough items for a minimal event, by all means add to it as resources allow. Grow your stockpiles and invest in survival gear little by little while you consider a more severe event. Primary items that follow are bare necessities that everyone should have to be prepared for a minimal event.

Make sure you have this list covered first, then move on to secondary items as you are able to afford them, securing your future when things get really grim.

Food for Preppers

Your main concern when prepping should be cultivating your stockpiles of nonperishable food and water. Even if you have very little to spend, you can still start small and simply add an item or two when grocery shopping to put away for hard times. Having extra items in the pantry that will keep for months or even years is always a smart investment, as you can fall back on your extra supplies in the event of a job loss or unexpected expense.

This makes prepping even more relevant to those who have little in the way of disposable income. If you do seem to have more time than money, you could certainly try your hand at canning/preserving foods at home as well. It is relatively inexpensive to start with and can help you take full advantage of the bounty of your garden or the frugality of buying in bulk. Make sure as your stockpile grows that you check expiration dates and rotate items to be consumed first to the front of your storage.

You'll only have to do this about every three months as long as you save items with a shelf life *longer* than that. The best way to extend the shelf life beyond the suggested "use by" date is to store food in cool temperatures away from sunlight. There are lots of items available that keep for a really long time, and they often end up being some of the cheapest! Most of the suggested foods that follow are ideal for tossing in the trusty bugout bag as well, just be sure to select ones that are lightweight and preferably ready to eat.

- Rice
- Beans
- Potatoes
- Matzo bread
- Canned seafood like tuna, sardines, salmon, trout and even octopus
- Bottled water
- Applesauce
- Granola bars
- Nuts
- Canned vegetables like green beans, corn and tomatoes
- Canned fruits like peaches, pineapple and fruit cocktail
- Hearty canned soups that don't require additional water
- Juice boxes
- Fruit snacks
- Beef jerky and beef sticks
- Honey
- Peanut butter singles
- Canned cheese
- Canned chicken
- Instant mashed potatoes
- Evaporated milk
- Dried fruit such as raisins, banana chips, apricots and prunes
- Fruit preserves

- Fruit leather
- Saltines
- Spam
- Graham crackers

Hygiene and Medical Care

No matter how careful you are in your day to day life, you will occasionally get sick or suffer a minor injury. And that's fine as long as you can pick up medicine at the store and visit the doctor when you need help. But during an emergency or an extended crisis your options become limited. You're going to have to play doctor now.

It is widely recommended to have a basic medical kit in your home kept for emergencies, and you can even buy preassembled kits in a vast range of sizes. These are handy because they are self-contained and you can grab it when you need it and have everything at hand. Most likely one of these would be sufficient to get you through a short lived disaster in which you are bugging in at home. But there may be other items you would like to add to your kit if you have certain medical conditions, or for the possibility of having to bug out.

If you are planning on being self-reliant for the long haul, carefully consider how you would handle a more serious injury. Treating broken limbs, deep lacerations or even gunshot wounds are not within the parameters of your little drugstore kit. There are other kits available out there which are based on military grade medical supplies. You will most likely have to search online for one of these, and they are definitely a little more expensive.

Even buying one of these may not cover everything you personally need. What you *should* do is review all the supplies available to you and customize a list to suit your needs. The items listed are simple suggestions to help you determine what should be in your home kit and your bugout bag.

- Ibuprofen- relieves pain, swelling *and* fevers
- Antibacterial ointment- keep your cuts and sores *clean*
- Bandages in various sizes
- Gauze, medical tape and scissors
- Fabric bandage for sprains- you have to stay mobile when you bugout
- Splint- fractured limbs need to be immobilized
- Hydrocortisone- an anti-itch cream can save you from bug bites, poison ivy and all kinds of skin rashes and allergic reactions

- Aloe and sunscreen- bugging out means you're going to be in the sun, you can even get a sunburn in winter conditions, so protect yourself when possible
- Tweezers- you may find a nasty splinter or a pesky wood tick
- Antibacterial wipes or hand sanitizer- whatever you're doing, try to keep clean
- Antidiarrheal medication- think about *this* when you're living in the woods
- Antacids and anti-gas capsules- these are simply to ease discomfort, but keeping comfortable can improve morale
- Aspirin- pain reliever commonly used for people at risk of heart attacks
- Antifungal cream- just in case all your hard, sweaty work leads to athlete's foot or jock itch, fungus is *not* going to go away on its own
- Hot shower bag- check these out for a super cool camping accessory, definitely will improve morale and hygiene
- Bleach tablets and iodine- can help purify water and sanitize instruments
- Tourniquet- you've got to stop the bleeding if you want to keep your people
- Hydrogen peroxide- can be used to flush out wounds or as mouthwash

- Garlic is famous for its antibacterial and antimicrobial properties, can cure colds when ingested – you can even apply it topically or near an infected area
- Vitamins
- Animal antibiotics- fish antibiotics include penicillin, amoxicillin and clindamycin which is helpful if you learn the proper dosages
- Prednisone may be helpful to reduce allergic reactions such as inflammation, but it is tricky figuring out how to begin doses and taper them off

- Sleep aids- to be used with caution
- N95 face masks- filters out particles in the air, can even help with seasonal allergies
- Feminine products
- Toothpaste, toothbrush and floss
- Bucket with a toilet lid and lots of plastic bags
- Extra pair of prescription lenses
- Extra prescribed medications

Remember that expiration dates on medication are only the guarantee the manufacturer wants to uphold, and almost all medicines aside from liquids and those requiring refrigeration can last two to five years with almost full potency. You can safely stockpile more medicine than you can use up in a year, as long as you rotate your stock and use up the oldest items first.

Your Bugout Bag

Every prepper needs to have a bugout bag, also called a go bag or 72 hour bag. The purpose of your bugout bag is to have enough supplies to live off of for at least three days in a pre-packed bag that you can just grab and go. If things aren't safe at home anymore, you should be able to just drop everything and rely on the backpack you placed by the door.

Everyone's bag is different, as everyone's needs and environment are different. When you pack your supplies, consider the climate, terrain and your target destination. When you're on your own, your mission is to secure food, water and shelter. Most people bring too much stuff, and exceed the amount they can comfortably carry.

The rule of thumb is to keep your bag to 25% of your total body weight, and that is if you are generally healthy and fit. Hiking for a few miles with your bag will tell you if it's too heavy, in which case you will have to remove some items or replace them with lighter ones. There are many ultralight items which are being made to serve this purpose, as well as tools that combine several items into one.

So whether you have a military knapsack, mountaineering bag or a plain old backpack, test its weight and keep improving it as you go. Many times there's something you really want to bring, but it's not considered essential for life. If you are with other people, everyone can carry a few different specialized items, as you will only need one for the entire group. In the end,, it's all up to you when you pack your bugout bag. The items that follow are main essentials for surviving outside the home, and you will decide to add or delete items as you go.

- A few snacks, like granola bars, beef jerky or trail mix
- A full water bottle with an included filter
- Nonperishable items such as canned goods or MRE's (meals ready to eat)
- Small metal cup or pot for cooking and collecting water
- Ultralight sleeping bag or bedroll
- Reflective emergency blanket
- Plastic sheeting, duct tape and rope or paracord for shelter, or an ultralight tent
- Two ways of making fire, such as a lighter, waterproof matches and a flint striker
- Compass and map of surrounding area
- Basic medical kit
- High quality survival knife
- Handgun and extra ammunition
- A change of clothes
- Multi-tool with can opener
- Signaling mirror or flares
- Hand sanitizer and cleansing cloths
- Toilet paper, to use sparingly

- Rain poncho can be used to keep you or your pack dry
- Flashlight, either handheld or worn on the head
- Several baggies to keep small items safe and dry

A Word on Knives

You're not going to get far in any survival situation without a good knife. A knife is by far the most useful and versatile tool available, and this is why many people carry a small pocket knife with them everywhere they go. Aside from violence, which may be necessary in an act of self-defense, a knife can provide you with a means of cutting, splitting, prying or even digging. Any knife is better than none, but while we're out shopping, what all needs to be considered?

First, let's examine the difference between a folding blade and a fixed blade. A folding blade is small and easy to carry, you can comfortably bring a means of survival with you every day, wherever you go. Go for a Swiss Army style, with all of its attachments, and you're ready for anything. Small odd jobs can be accomplished with your folding blade, no worries. But a blade that folds is weaker, and can't hold up to heavy duty tasks or battle.

The joint in the folding blade is a weak spot that will eventually give and break. A fixed blade is one piece of metal that will absorb energy evenly and is far more durable. If you're aiming to cut through wood or stab an attacker, you'll need the reliability of a fixed blade. Since they don't fold, they take up more space and should be carried in an appropriate sheath. Perhaps it's best to keep a folding blade in your pocket and bugout bag, while relying on your fixed blade when you need something more stable – or threatening.

The other factor in the strength of your knife is the *tang* – the length of the actual piece of metal the blade is constructed from. A full tang blade will reach past the hilt and all the way down the handle, and this is definitely what you should be looking for. If your blade stops where the handle starts or tapers off into the handle, it will eventually break. Like the joint in a folding knife, the point where the metal ends creates a weak spot. If you see a pretty knife and it's on the cheaper side, determine whether it is full tang or not. If not, you may need to keep looking.

For functionality and ease of use, choose a knife that ends in a sharp, *pointed* tip. There are many different shapes for blade edges and ends, but what you as a *prepper* are looking for is reliability, not style. If you need to cut or stab into something, a pointed end will be the easiest to pull back out. Serrations, holes and curves can increase the likelihood of your knife becoming lodged in your target, and you may need your knife back!

Choosing a knife with a pointed tip will aid you in many survival tasks, such as picking at a splinter or loosening a screw when you have no other tools at your disposal. You can purchase and carry as many different blade styles as you like, but make sure you have a sharp point on your most prized and trusted knife.

Weapons Ready

Whether you like it or not, there may come a time when you need to defend yourself from a deadly attack. Despite your best efforts to fly under the radar and secure your perimeter, you now have a violent intruder breaking into your home. What will you do now?

In a prolonged survival situation, hiding may not be enough and you may have to fight to stay alive. The threat will come with no regard for your law abiding, peaceful nature – and you're not going to be able to negotiate with a bear in your campsite or a zombie on your lawn. You *must* arm yourself to survive, even if you tell yourself you'll never raise your weapon. Fine. Don't. But how about you bring a weapon along just in case you change your mind?

Firearms

Having a gun at the ready during your worst nightmare scenario can really improve your odds of survival. If someone is set on threatening your right to survive, just point and shoot, like a camera! It really is terrible that such a weapon exists that can take a person off this planet so easily and thoughtlessly.

But we are preparing for a prolonged disaster, where people will take the law into their own hands – it's best you have a weapon like a firearm to quickly get you out of danger if the situation really does call for it. You don't need a million guns, just one or two would do nicely. In reality you don't need more guns than you have people to fire them. If you want to stockpile something, amass large quantities of ammo for your weapons.

Keeping your chosen firearms in only a few calibers will keep things simple for the people utilizing your armory. If you just appreciate guns and fancy yourself a collector, go ahead and explore your passion, but decide on allocating certain purchases for use when it really does hit the fan.

Handguns – Many people simply keep a handgun in the home just in case someone breaks in at night, and this is a good place to start. All handguns are easily carried and operated, and are definitely lethal, especially in close quarters. Every person in the home should be trained on using it safely.

The main point in gun safety is to *always* treat a gun as if it were loaded. Never ever point a gun at something or someone you do not wish to shoot. Accidents happen all the time, so keep that muzzle pointed down and away. Since a handgun is so easy to shoot, households with children should definitely keep it under lock and key in a place inaccessible to them.

Locking away your weapon will also prevent an intruder from getting to it before *you* do. You may decide locking it up and hiding it away will keep you from reaching it in time when someone breaks in. Lots of folks say they keep a handgun right on their nightstand, next to their bed. For safety's sake, you should at least have it out unloaded, and stash your loaded clip nearby – maybe tuck it behind your nightstand or in your sock drawer. Get creative!

Remember that purchasing any gun is an investment. Common reliable handguns range from about $250 to $500, and definitely sell higher as well. Do your homework before you buy. Read articles on different handguns. Visit retail locations to inspect certain types that call to you. Ask the person at the counter to take one or several out for you, and if they can tell you more about it.

It is important to handle several guns before deciding on one, it is paramount that it feel comfortable in *your* hands. Some handguns will be too big, too small, too heavy or too light for you to fire them effectively. Everyone has their opinion on which handgun is superior, but it's just the one that works best for them. What will work best for *you*?

Talk to fellow gun owners and ask about their selection. If they happen to be a friend of yours, they might take you out to the shooting range and you could even try their guns out before committing to a purchase. You will have to consider different trigger pulls, single or double action handguns and magazine capacities, but get a *feel* for them and carry the handgun that fits you.

Shotguns – A homeowner wielding a shotgun would make any invader think twice. We see the awesome power of this weapon in movies, tearing people apart at close range. It's not a bad idea to keep one around, but it definitely has its drawbacks. It takes a little more muscle and training to handle a weapon that offers this much power.

Perhaps you have seen videos online of people firing a shotgun for the first time – the kickback can knock you right over! Another consideration is how often the shotgun can potentially jam. This tends to happen a bit more with the automatic version, so as long as you can manage a pump action successfully you should probably stick with one of those, at least initially.

You're going to have to clear that jam during combat, and make your shots count. Also, a shotgun isn't only going to destroy your enemy, it's probably going to destroy your house as well. Projectiles could pass all the way through your target, so make sure of what's behind them or next to them before unloading.

Shotguns are also great at attracting unwanted attention, as they are extremely loud. Unless your position has been thoroughly compromised and you need serious crowd control, select another firearm.

Rifles – A rifle is suited for long range attacks, securing your perimeter and even hunting for food. A lookout with a scoped rifle can eliminate threats at a distance or at least buy you extra time to address the situation and bugout if necessary.

AR-15s have become insanely popular with preppers, as they are fairly easy to handle and you can expend lots of rounds quickly. They're not necessarily cheap though – you're going to have to save up for this one. Combat with a rifle at closer range can be dangerous, as the bullets could pass through people and walls.

Always maintain control when firing and resist the temptation to "spray and pray". In the hands of a disciplined shooter, this weapon is surely a problem solver.

Other Weapons

Yes, you should definitely invest in a firearm, at least one handgun to carry with you to get you out of a potentially deadly situation. But during your survival there are many alternatives that may serve you better. Save the guns as a last resort. They require special care and handling, and no matter what they make far more noise than you would ever want to. What other weapons can you add to your arsenal?

Combat Knife – Your main blade should be able to defend you in combat. In addition to other blade requirements, it should be long enough to reach the enemy and deal penetrating damage. However, its length should not make it cumbersome or difficult to wield in close quarters. In cramped spaces, you may be able to attack with your knife before the enemy can draw his gun on you and fire. Carry your knife in an easily accessible place on your body and practice drawing it from the sheath quickly and safely. Practicing will lead to muscle memory, which can bring an advantage when your adrenaline takes over.

Machete – Is bigger better? Sometimes, yes! Carrying a machete can improve your range in a fight, and the sight of one may make a would-be attacker think twice. As with any blade, your machete can also be a valuable tool and you should aim to purchase one of high quality and strength.

Crossbow – The draw of this weapon is range and stealth. Firing a bolt from a crossbow gives you a ranged attack like a firearm would. And unlike a firearm you can shoot in silence instead of drawing attention to your location. Being able to retrieve and reuse your ammunition is a significant perk of this weapon. Skilled archers can enjoy all of these benefits with a regular bow as well, the crossbow just makes it a little easier with its simple point and shoot action.

Crowbar – Ah yes, the satisfaction and reliability of blunt force. You could also reach for a medieval mace or a baseball bat if you like, but the crowbar is just straight up useful. The crowbar's appeal lies in its ability to function as a tool, which is what it is actually made for. Every group who is bugging out should probably have one for gaining entry to barricaded areas or stored items. As a weapon you can swing and bash the bad guy in, thrust at the enemy like a spear or hook them with the curved edge. All of these options have definitely made the crowbar a favorite among zombie preppers, who focus on targeting the head.

Non-Lethal Irritants – Pepper spray or mace can give you an advantage in combat or make it possible to flee. If you are unable to legally obtain pepper spray you can brew up our own at home, just ask the internet! Gel based irritants work exceptionally well because they cling to the attacker, instead of the wind blowing it back into your own eyes.

In a true survival situation, you may not be as concerned about using substances that don't do permanent damage. In that case, any sprayed chemical will do the job for you by creating distance and temporarily *or* permanently blinding your attacker. For example, investigate the wide assortment of insect repellants available on the market. Some aerosol sprays designed to kill bugs inside the home have a very focused stream, and sprays meant for taking out wasp nests will definitely give you the range you need to stay safe.

In the old days, ninjas used finely ground glass blown into an enemy's eyes to destroy his sight. Anything in the eyes is going to slow your opponent down, for sure. But if you do decide you want something that only incapacitates and does not *harm* an enemy, go grab a high capacity squirt gun and try out some do-it-yourself concoctions. At the very least it should be a memorable afternoon.

Incendiaries – For the record, you should avoid fighting with fire whenever possible. Flames are not something you can easily control, and can quickly spread to structures or property you do not wish to burn. Flamethrowers, Molotov cocktails and other fiery weapons will definitely draw attention and make a mess of things. Whether to use flames in combat should be left up to the most level-headed, conservative person in your group. If you do want to explore the creation of incendiaries, a prepper might want to keep some lighter fluid or alcohol-based sanitizer around. Hand sanitizer is especially cheap, flammable and easy to carry. You may be able to squirt it out of the bottle onto the enemy or coat projectiles with it. At the very least, it should help when you're having trouble getting a campfire going.

Tools and Other Gear

You never know what you may encounter in a survival situation. Maybe you're bugging in and decide to board up the windows. Maybe you bugged out on your mountain bike and it's in need of repair. Or you've been living in the forest for the past month and you want to fashion a spear for hunting.

Between your home, your bugout bag and your survival caches you may want to add tools and other gear to help you through tough situations and solve problems. Consider what you might want to add to your supplies as space and weight restrictions allow. The following items are mainly supplemental to your other preps. Anything considered to be mandatory will also be found in the other supply lists.

- Multi-tool – They come in all shapes and sizes, and you can acquire one or several to cover your bases.

- Flashlight – You will absolutely need light when the power goes out. In addition to the traditional flashlight you can also use a lantern or strap on a head lamp to keep your hands free.

- Paracord – A strong length of parachute cord, often sold as woven bracelets that you can unravel when you need it. It will hold up as well as any rope and won't take up space in your bugout bag.

- Collapsible or multi-function shovel – Digging trenches will definitely be easier if you have an actual shovel. Camping shovels are collapsible and lightweight, allowing them to travel with you. Some shovels have sharp edges or serrations to perform other tasks, and some even have bottle openers!

- Duct tape – Duct tape can solve any problem. Whether you're patching the roof of your tent or building a raft, you're going to need duct tape.

- Multiple fire starters – Fire is key to staying fed and keeping warm. You should *always* have several ways of making fire in case you lose your lighter. Carry extra lighters as well as waterproof matches and a magnesium striker. Have fire starters with every jacket and bag, as well as in your car. Keep small batches of tinder as well – dryer lint smeared with petroleum jelly or a few pieces of char cloth stored in a medicine bottle or small tin will get your fire blazing fast.

- Compass and map of surrounding area – If you bug out into the thick of the wilderness or into the next town, it can't hurt to have a guide of the area. Having a secondary location to bug out to is your ultimate goal, and you need to make sure everyone can get there even if they *think* they know the way.

- Small bags – Plastic sandwich baggies are great for keeping small items together and dry. There are also polyester bags available that will guarantee protection from water damage and make less noise. The polyester bags will also be reusable indefinitely.

- Sewing kit – A missing button is not that big of a deal, but in a prolonged survival situation your clothes may eventually be reduced to rags. Even without actual sewing *skills*, you can manage to patch up a few holes or stick a button on with some needle and thread. If you have the time, however, learn how to sew. It's definitely a prepper skill!

- Sleeping pad – When you bug out you can certainly sleep on the ground if you have to. You may opt for a sleeping bag or a bed roll that's as light as possible. A sleeping pad can keep you off the cold, wet ground and boost your comfort level. And when bugging in you may acquire a few guests, so consider having a sleeping pad or air mattress and some extra bedding in the home.

- Fasteners and binders – You don't want to burn through all your duct tape, right? Include some other little items like safety pins, elastic bands, key chain rings and zip ties. They won't add any weight or bulk to your bugout bag, and you can even carry them in your pockets if you like.

- Wearable items – Like paracord bracelets or the addition of some extra safety pins to your jacket, any tool you can wear will provide more room in the bugout bag – and make it far easier to access than rifling through your bag all the time. You can find small tools and flashlights that can be worn around the neck, and compasses get attached to just about everything imaginable. You can fashion your own necklace for an item or even hang small tools off of your belt. Just remember to keep it all functional, quiet and out of the way of your weapons.

- Two way radios – If you're traveling with a group or make a friend out there, you might want to or *have* to communicate at a distance. If you split up to find food or are patrolling your perimeter, having a radio can keep you efficient and keep you safe. Remember to keep your volume low, and silence your radio if you're being hunted.

- Plywood and nails – If you have a space to store some plywood, two by fours, hammer and nails, you'll definitely have an easier time in the long run. You can board up windows, build barricades, repair your structure or fashion a new one. If you have a garage or secondary location, it can be a smart investment for the apocalypse.

- Fire extinguisher – The last thing you need is for your house to burn to the ground when society has already collapsed around you. A perfectly good shelter with everything you need deserves to be maintained and protected. Always follow fire safety precautions, doomsday or not. You've worked hard for your supplies, take care of what's yours by keeping a fire extinguisher at your primary and secondary locations.

- Can openers – Just like fire starters, you should keep more than one can opener around in case one gets lost or it breaks. It doesn't take long for a manual cranking can opener to break or jam up. You should keep a couple of those in the home, but also use the military style can openers that can punch through metal. They are one piece of metal with no mechanisms to break, small and easy to tuck in a pocket or bag. And as far as cans go, buy the self-opening ones with the pull tab whenever possible.

- Generator – In many disasters it is possible your home will lose power. In the apocalypse, the power's not coming back anytime soon. Having a generator will keep your lights on and the refrigerator running. There are generators that run on multiple fuels or solar powered models, which can be a great backup.

- Rechargeable batteries and solar powered charger – When there's no electricity you're going to turn to your battery operated devices, especially flashlights. Rechargeable batteries have come a long way and last much longer than they used to. Having a solar charging station will keep them going, and you can also get solar chargers for cell phones and other small electrical items. If the sun's still coming up every morning, you might as well use it.

- Fuel and fuel pump – Cars and gasoline generators will require fuel or they will become useless junk. Stockpiling gasoline is doable, but requires appropriate storage space and rotation, as gas can deteriorate in as little as three months. There are additives to help the shelf life of your gasoline, but you should also have a siphon on hand when you need to scavenge for gas on the road.

- Activated charcoal – This stuff can be found in capsule form in the vitamin section of many stores. People ingest the capsules to purify their insides, but activated charcoal can purify just about anything – including the water you drink and the air you breathe. Filtering water through charcoal can help to decontaminate a found water source you need to drink from. You can even fashion your very own "gas masks" by layering face masks used for house painting with ground up charcoal, making it easier to breathe through airborne chemicals and particles.

- Hacksaw and bolt cutters – In addition to tightening screws or loosening nuts, you may have to cut through some stuff. There are some things you're not going to be able to cut through with your survival knife. Having a saw and cutters can help you build shelter or gain access through fences and chains.

- Heirloom seeds and gardening tools – If things get out of hand for too long, and you have to wait for society to rebuild itself, growing a garden can sustain you in the meantime. Having your own food means fewer supply runs that become less fruitful and more dangerous as time goes on. Keeping heirloom seeds will produce fruits and vegetables that develop new seeds for future planting. Study up on how to grow your own food and which plants are best suited for your climate.

- Candles – Everyone should have candles in case the power goes out, even if they think preppers are insane and there's nothing to prepare for. Tea light candles don't burn long but they are small, easy to carry and you can buy them in bulk. There are also long-burning candles which are usually coiled beeswax, which can last up to 60 hours. Just make sure you do have candles and use them safely, away from flammable items.

Clothes to Survive In

During times of survival, fashion takes a back seat to comfort and utility. Nobody is going to care if your clothes are wrinkled and your outfit doesn't match. Maintaining your personal comfort for as long as possible will keep you going through the tough stuff. Being appropriately dressed for your environment and keeping your body protected are vital and should be given consideration. It's definitely easier to select your wardrobe before a disaster, so keep these points in mind during your preps.

Footwear should be appropriate for long hikes and should already be broken in. You must be able to move at a moment's notice, and nothing will slow you down like blisters on your achy, tired feet.

Wearing layers will allow you to adapt to changing temperatures, and is especially recommended in cold weather over wearing one thicker layer. An example of an outfit for warm and cool temps might include a long sleeved shirt, undershirt, hooded weatherproof jacket with removable liner and pants that can also zip off to shorts.

Your hairstyle may undergo some changes if you find yourself in a prolonged battle for survival. What people find attractive is often not the most practical. Shorter hair definitely requires less brushing and detangling, not to mention harder for someone to grab you by and better for hotter climates. But before you go shaving your head realize that your scalp can definitely suffer from sunburn and may require sunscreen or a hat. In a colder climate longer hair can retain body heat even better than just a hat, although both would be ideal.

Utility and protection are your main concerns. Sunglasses and a handkerchief will aid you whether it is hot or cold outside. Sporting a belt could save a life later if someone needs a tourniquet. Work gloves can save your hands when you're climbing a jagged mountainside or collecting firewood. A jacket or vest for tactical purposes or outdoor recreation will provide you with plenty of pockets to carry all your little survival tools and free up space in your backpack.

Keeping a Low Profile

Whether you're bugging in at home or making camp out in the wilderness, keeping a low profile is your best defense. There may be looters, gangs or even the undead out on the prowl, and you may not be equipped to take them all on. You should always sweep your perimeter for potential threats, but try to do so without drawing attention. The best way to get noticed is to be seen and heard, so unless you're flagging down a rescue helicopter, try to remain undetected.

<u>Be Invisible</u> – Make sure you see them before they see you. Try to wear drab, muted colors and if possible match them to the colors of your surroundings. Camouflage comes in many different color patterns to lower visibility in different terrains. Traditional green forest camo isn't going to help you in the snow or the desert. Some people even construct ghillie suits, which are outfits matching the color of your terrain and have the surrounding natural vegetation added to them.

The purpose of these suits is to blend into the environment and break up the recognizable outline of the human body. Whatever you decide to wear, avoid bright, contrasting colors if you want to avoid detection. Sadly, if you've just dyed your hair bright neon blue, you're going to stand out in all the wrong ways. You'll have to cover your hair up when you're out in the open. Maybe you could just shave your head and start over!

Take off anything sparkly or flashy that could reflect the sun's rays, such as a wristwatch or a shiny gold necklace. At home, cover your windows – with blackout curtains if possible. At night, use low light or no light if you can get by without it. When there's no power and you *do* need light, keep it dim with a small tea light candle or even a glow stick if that's all you need. If you have a basement or other room without windows, you can use it for your nighttime tasks where light is necessary.

Disable any motion detectors or timers on your lights at home – you are not trying to scare off a petty burglar anymore, you are trying to conceal yourself from extremely dangerous and violent criminals in what might be an abandoned neighborhood! When bugging out, make a fire when you must for cooking or warmth, but keep it small and have someone posted as lookout until you can extinguish it.

If you just need a fire for cooking, relocate and sleep in a different area when you are done. Maybe you can do without a fire for warmth by using reflective emergency blankets that will trap the heat from your body. If you are with other people, consider them a resource and by all means snuggle up together for warmth. You might not even like each other, but be prepared to get a *little* uncomfortable if you want to survive!

<u>Be Quiet</u> – Reduce noise by speaking softly and whisper when you suspect danger. Avoid wearing chains or jewelry and remove loose change or keys from your pockets. You can even remove zipper pulls from jackets and backpacks to reduce noise while moving.

Silence your handgun or opt for a combat knife or machete to defend yourself while patrolling. Mute cell phones, radios, home phones and even alarm clocks that may go off at inopportune moments. Does your wristwatch have an alarm? You'd better disable it. Control your reactions and resist crying out in surprise.

Maybe a mouse skittered over your foot, or you tripped over a log and fell. Scan the path you are walking as well as looking ahead to avoid being startled. If the baby is crying and you know danger is close, your best option may be to flick a few drops of water in their face – it doesn't hurt them and has been known to snap them right out of it. Finally, have medicines on hand to stop coughs and sneezes when stealth is required. You have to be quiet when it counts.

A Survival Mentality

Your outlook on a situation alone can determine whether you survive. There are countless stories of people who endured the impossible with no sign of rescue, but they never gave up hope. You have to believe that your situation may change, keeping your mind active and positive.

In a worst case scenario you may find yourself starving, freezing, or dealing with a crippling injury, but your attitude towards your predicament will determine how your story ends. Fight for your life, always look for opportunities to improve your situation- *believe* that you will make it through.

You will have to rely on your wits and endurance if you go it alone, but what if you have someone there by your side? Your chances of surviving can improve with other people, but they must also have the right mindset. When times get tough, you will have to lift each other up. Enduring a harsh existence for any prolonged amount of time can make a person just want to give up.

Let's face facts. Someone in your group may have an emotional breakdown from exhaustion, starvation, dehydration, isolation, boredom, anxiety, missing friends or relatives or even witnessing a death. Physical discomfort from small things such as sweating, chafing, itching, muscle fatigue, headaches and not bathing can take a considerable toll after awhile, and not everyone is as strong as you are.

They're thinking about hot showers, home cooked meals and video games. They don't want to walk another mile, they don't want to spend another night going hungry. You can't change the circumstances you are in. What else can you do to improve their situation?

- Distract from discomfort by stopping to do a gear check or gathering resources like firewood.
- Play a mental game like I Spy or Twenty Questions.
- Give them a sip of water.
- Have something to read to take their focus off the situation.
- Sing to them and have them join in.
- Bring physical comfort by holding them, giving hugs or scratching their back. When you make camp you might even trade foot massages. Whatever feels good!
- Let them cry or break down for a moment to release their frustrations.
- Compromise – agree to rest for a few minutes before climbing that next hill. Let them take first watch so they can have uninterrupted sleep for the night.
- Point out all the positives in whatever you're doing, and make them feel like they've really gotten something when you bargain with them.

- Taking some action, even if it doesn't solve the problem, may still have a positive effect in that there is a sense of accomplishment and control.
- Letting them come up with a solution on their own might boost their confidence as well, when they are feeling so helpless.
- A person suffering from withdrawals of any substance is going through a lot, give them lots of praise for how well they are doing and occupy their mind when cravings take hold.
- Just simply talk to them and remind them of what is necessary from all of you to survive.

<u>Items for Trade</u>

Certain disasters may not be over quickly. A complete economic collapse, an EMP event, or a worldwide zombie infestation will change your day to day life considerably. You've been prepping, taking care of you and yours- how else can you make yourself useful?

If you wind up living in an apocalypse, having what others need can definitely improve your situation. Having certain items to barter and trade with could prolong your existence considerably. Eventually everyone will have to resort to scavenging for supplies in homes, warehouses, and abandoned stores. As these areas are cleared out, people will become desperate for supplies.

With your stockpiles you can help others, obtain items you need – and possibly even make a deal for your life if you fall prey to marauders. These bartering items are a little different from your other preps. They are mainly comfort items, addictive substances that people crave, and some are essentials for people in certain situations.

If you can discipline yourself to exist without these crutches and niceties, you stand to profit when the world ends. (Learning to live with less is an essential prepper skill.) Even if you are on a limited budget, you can still accumulate a few of these items- you may want to just specialize in one or two. You can also hold off on purchasing these items and simply be on the lookout when you wake up in the apocalypse, seeing these treasures for what they really are.

- Coffee, caffeine pills, energy drinks and shots
- Cigarettes and alcohol
- Chocolate – other sweets as well, especially since chocolate can melt or go stale, but that's why it will be a rare treat and a huge morale booster
- Quality soaps and moisturizers, fresh razors, shampoo (save those bottles from the hotel), lip balm, sunscreen
- Extra clothing such as cotton tees and socks
- Baby items like diapers, baby wipes and formula
- Quality toilet paper, feminine napkins and tampons
- Medicine for colds and seasonal allergies, pain relievers, bandages and multivitamins
- Gasoline, propane and motor oil
- Lighters, flashlights and batteries

Hidden Caches

In case of a bugout situation it may be wise to have hidden caches of supplies near your home, on the way to your target destination, and at your target destination. Items can be stored in a weatherproof container for future access, usually buried in the ground or concealed in a secret spot that is well camouflaged.

These stores should only be emergency supplies to replace what may have been consumed or left behind. If you were forced to abandon your home or your supplies were stolen or destroyed, a cache can keep you going for a few days. Your biggest collection of backup supplies should be in the vicinity of your bugout location, where you plan to regroup, make camp and fortify your base.

There are many containers available to consider for your cache, the most economical would be a plastic container with a snap on lid. Contents inside your container which are perishable or vulnerable to the elements should be placed in sealed plastic bags. To further protect your supplies you should seal your container with duct tape before burying or concealing it. Consider how easy it will be to retrieve your items.

If you bury the cache, you must be able to get at it, even if you lose your shovel or the ground is frozen. You should do your best to cover the spot with materials natural to the area, such as branches, tall grasses or rocks. Make sure it looks natural, no obvious signs of a manmade, precise layout of material. However you hide it, you must make sure that no one else will possibly discover it.

You will lose your supplies and could potentially give away your location to looters. While you must hide your container well, you must also ensure that you WILL be able to find it again! What could be worse than being in a desperate situation on the run and having what you need but not being able to retrieve it? Pick a location you are familiar with or become very well acquainted with this location.

Maybe you have a secluded spot in the woods which is off the path, or you know of an abandoned field which is not appropriate for development. Your spot should be well known to you, but not to others. Find something off trail, in the rough, concealed with natural vegetation.

Your emergency cache should ideally be within a day's hike from your home. Walk to this location from your home, take different routes and really KNOW the way to your supplies. A map can certainly help and you may share your cache location with the trusted people you plan to bugout with.

Obviously if there are changes to your group you may wish to relocate your cache if you fear they may steal or sabotage your supplies- only tell who you must. The primary items listed would be appropriate for your emergency bugout cache which you would visit after leaving your home or desperately needed a resupply while bugging in. The secondary items are a great reserve to include in additional caches further out, on your way to your backup location.

PRIMARY CACHE ITEMS

- Toilet paper, wrapped in plastic – small items can be stored in the tubes
- Bottled water and canteen
- Water purification tablets or filter
- Nonperishable food, also a can opener if including canned items
- Duplicate of your primary medical kit
- Lighter, waterproof matches and char cloth/dryer lint
- Paracord
- Multi-tool
- Compass and map of surrounding area
- Survival knife for camping/outdoors which can double as a combat knife
- Ammunition for bugout firearm(s)
- Flashlight
- Duct tape
- Pair of socks

SECONDARY CACHE ITEMS

- Heirloom seeds which when planted will produce new seeds
- Flares and signaling mirror

- Batteries for any flashlights or other devices you may use or find in the future
- More toilet paper, food and water, you can never have enough
- Small toolkit including screwdrivers, pliers, and a wire saw
- Solar powered or hand crank radio
- Survival/pocket knife
- Backup weapon such as a combat knife, machete, crowbar
- Tarp or plastic sheeting for rudimentary protection from the elements
- Container for gathering and boiling water
- Compact shovel
- Secondary medical kit

Drills and Dry Runs

You may find it beneficial to implement some survival drills, so that when the time comes you know exactly what you need to do and how to get it done efficiently. Even the simplest thing like knowing where your family will meet up in the event of a house fire can be a disaster if you don't discuss it beforehand and try it out.

Everyone involved must be in agreement, move quickly and decisively, and know the possible pitfalls and obstacles. What harm is there in conducting a drill? Absolutely none, do NOT feel silly for trying to ensure your continued survival! If you and your loved ones know exactly what to do when a tornado siren goes off or there is a citywide blackout, you already have a distinct advantage in a disaster, even if you do not stock extra supplies.

Your neighbors will say they don't have time for a plan and a drill, or that the disaster will never happen. You should do your best to make sure your people aren't the ones running around lost in a panic, terrified and vulnerable- make a plan! Not to mention that out of all the prepping you may do, practicing safety drills is the cheapest. You don't need equipment, hoarded supplies or funding, it is free. So, what sort of questions do we need to answer when considering a survival drill?

- Which events should you bug in for and which should you bug out for? For instance, you will probably be bugging in during a tornado and bugging out during a fire.

- What supplies do you need to grab and where will they be located? You may want to grab a flashlight and a radio if heading to your basement. If you need to leave, bugout bags should be prepped and in place.

- Where can the members of your household/group meet up if your home is compromised and you need to bug out? Maybe head for the street light at the corner, your neighbor's yard, or the gas station a few blocks away. You MUST be in agreement on this, and it should be idiot-proof- not "100 yards past the big oak tree and then 50 paces west". Pick a landmark you all know that even a child left on their own could find.

- What can you do to protect your home during the disaster? In the event of looting and riots you should lock doors, cover windows and prepare to barricade entry points. If your house is threatened by wildfires, you should close your windows and start watering your roof. Visualize the disaster and what it will *threaten*.

- What can you do to protect yourselves during the disaster? Do your children know how to call 911 and what they should say? Is there a firearm in the house and is everyone trained on proper handling and use?

- What sort of dry runs would help you prepare? How long would it take you to pack everyone in the van and drive to the nearest grocery store? What will it be like when you have to help each other into the hazmat suits? Just what exactly is it going to take to get your survival raft inflated and in the water?

Every step you take towards preparedness will make you a strong and skilled survivor. Remember why you are doing these drills. You can "look stupid" doing dry runs and making your family run around for nothing, or you can *definitely* look stupid when you stand helpless in horror as it finally hits the fan. Don't be that guy.

Well, there you have it.

Hopefully reviewing these tips will make you a more confident and successful prepper. In the end your own ingenuity and growing knowledge will keep you alive in any situation and will cost you very little. Focus on learning skills and practicing techniques with what you have, while aiming to save for tomorrow.

Read about prepping and all kinds of stories of survival. Get out there and meet some fellow preppers as well. Most of them are happy to give advice and share a few of their secrets. Without a sense of community, we will be truly lost in the wake of devastation. Some of us will have to work to rebuild society and lend a helping hand to those in need, which makes prepping a most noble hobby indeed.

Hopefully nothing bad will ever happen to you, but if things do take a turn for the worse, you *can* survive!

Good luck, fellow preppers!

*****

If you've enjoyed this book, **please** consider leaving a review and letting others know what you thought!

www.ingramcontent.com/pod-product-compliance
Lightning Source LLC
Chambersburg PA
CBHW070826290526
45795CB00002B/847